ONE MAN'S
JOURNEY
FROM THE DARKNESS
INTO THE LIGHT

ONE MAN'S
JOURNEY
FROM THE DARKNESS
INTO THE LIGHT

ANDREW S MAJORS

Kravitz & Sons
INNOVATORS IN PUBLISHING, MARKETING AND ADVERTISING

Kravitz and Sons LLC
204 E Arlington Blvd. Suite B
Greenville, NC 27858

Published by Kravitz and Sons LLC.

ISBN: 979-8-89639-472-3 (sc)
ISBN: 979-8-89639-471-6 (e)

Library of Congress Control Number: 2024927532

TABLE OF CONTENTS

PART ONE

INTRODUCTION

After my turbulent teen years, I realized quitting high school was a mistake. I then got my GED and made a half-hearted effort at College. Though I had been reading self-help and self-improvement independently, I had not yet considered how closely these readings intertwined with my college studies in the behavioral sciences. In this way, I was becoming self-educated in a field that was largely uncharted at this time. Education is acquiring knowledge, whereas experience and suffering are the mothers of wisdom.

So as things evolved and came about, I grew from a down and out vagrant and bordered on being a societal dreg to a strong, contributing benefactor to several different members of various cultures in "The Melting Pot" our part of the world.

Of course, to me, it was a fair exchange between me helping others adapt to their new environment and learning new ways and ideas as to how to flourish in my own world and homeland. It became apparent to me that I can be different, without changing and accepting another's attitudes and behaviors. Apples and oranges are different although they are both fruit and can be enjoyed equally.

It's better to walk alone, than with a crowd going in the wrong direction.

Surround yourself with those on the same mission as you!

I guess it's okay and a reasonably safe assumption to say that I was gaining an identity and philosophy along with attitudes beneficial to a wide array of the world's various people and that was enriching to me and my people, thus joining in and helping on a number of fronts.

To me, that makes it safe to say that the more I benefitted others, the more I became a much stronger and better person.

Knowledge is knowing a tomato is a fruit; wisdom is not putting a tomato in a fruit salad! Nuggets like these and my insights gained in psychotherapy, Zen meditation, and my spiritual disciplines have taught me that a fish should not be expected to climb a tree any more than a man can be expected to fly without assistance.

So, you think that religion should be taugh in schoos? Would that be all religions? ...Or just yours?

You can watch me, mock me, block me, or join me. What you cannot do is stop me.

To this end, as an introduction to my metamorphosis and insight as an individual, I present two statements to align my thinking and purpose: As I undertook the challenge to grow, I thought of the phrase, "Bloom where you're planted!" Many of us believe we must change our surroundings to improve within ourselves, but this is rarely the case.

When your vision is operating on a higher level than your surroundings expect to be misunderstood & talked about

"Here's to the crazy ones. The misfits. The rebels. The trou-ble-makers. The round pegs in the square holes. The ones who see things differently. They're not fond of rules, and they have no respect for the status-quo. You can quote them, disagree with them, glorify, or vilify them. But the only thing you can't do is ignore them. Because they change things. They push the human race forward. And while some may see them as the crazy ones, we see genius. Because the people who are crazy enough to think they can change the world, are the ones who do."

Being a fan of R&B, the lyrics to the song "Man in the Mirror" struck a positive chord. I realized that the least expensive and most effective way to grow would be to stop the poor and negative behaviors

that were getting me into trouble. By coincidence, I found an excellent book for those trying to change their attitudes and behavior.

This book was Positive Addiction by Dr. William Glasser, head of the Harvard Department of Psychiatry. In this book, Glasser informs us through scientific studies that when trying to eliminate a negative attitude and behavior, the odds of success increase when we supplant the undesirable with something positive.

At this point in my life, I often admired people who had success in being combative, and this admiration contributed to erroneously thinking that violence was the best way to solve problems. After having several scuffles, I pursued martial arts, namely karate and jiujitsu training from the military. I mastered the basics with years of participation and got a first-degree black belt. At that time, I had ceased all drug use. Wanting to broaden my martial arts experience, I began practicing jiujitsu and zen meditation for physical and mental awareness.

Continued growth of the man in the mirror

The idea of blooming where planted and being responsible for the man in the mirror reminds me of the expression, "Attitudes are contagious. Is yours worth catching?"

I have seen that no belief system or reasoning is impervious to alternatives. Even so, some ways of thinking have so much strength and resilience that, over time, they become common sense. At times, these beliefs may be flawed or even inapplicable, but the idea that love and peace can help us overcome hardship and differences has shown to be more valuable than its exceptions.

~ ~ ~

THIS IS HOW YOUR LIGHT CAN CHANGE THE WORLD.

Part Two

How a Small, Positive Thought grew into a magnificent obsession

I heard often throughout my life that from tiny acorns, giant oaks do grow. I always knew that significant things could come from a small beginning. No matter how far you have traveled, your journey has to start somewhere. Lao Tzu elucidates this by saying, "A journey of a thousand miles began with one step."

When I wanted to help my family with adverse decisions such as mind-altering drugs, knowing where to start left me bewildered.

A friend had seen my earlier attempts to become a writer and suggested I write something for children. Something clicked when she said that, and I promptly put that inspiration into motion.

I didn't know anything about writing children's books then, so I researched how to write for beginning readers at the library—I refused to let my lack of know-how interfere with my enthusiasm.

One of my influences, Normal Vincent Peal, who popularized positive thinking, said, "Enthusiasm makes the difference!" This statement also served as the title of the book. This phrase means that approaching any significant matter with enthusiasm can be the difference between success and failure.

Just as the giant Oak grows from a tiny acorn with the inherent desire to reach its full potential but may do better with some help, I wanted to help my daughter and now grandchildren reach their potential through positive guidance and decision-making.

By reading and expanding my horizons, I acquired a much broader perspective through the acquisition of such aphorisms as "To the child who doesn't read, the world is a closed book." Also, "If you want to hide something from a fool, put it in a book."

As my enthusiasm grew, my desire to positively influence others also grew. Starting from the man in the mirror and then my family, I have reached the point of disseminating the wisdom gained from experiences and metamorphosis.

Even though I had grown, evolved my attitude, and had more enthusiasm than ever, some of those around me projected their negativity onto me because of my previous behavior. My new ways of thinking and behaving were sometimes in conflict with their entrenched way of seeing things.

This memory reminds me of a phrase on my high school football stadium, "Have I improved today?" I took this further and asked myself, how can I improve today? Yesterday is a canceled check; tomorrow is a promissory note. We have only today to spend, so we must spend wisely. Nothing can change what has passed, but through introspection, we can use today to improve upon the past. By living fully today, we can make for a better tomorrow.

All this is to say that my journey of being an author of materials written to help all people elevate their lives has evolved from wanting to help my family. While it is not always easy to make changes to improve the wonderful gift called life, it is impossible without putting in continuous effort.

Seeing the miraculous transformation of a caterpillar into a beautiful butterfly is still not as dramatic as what the human experience can reveal to us over time. I say this because individuals can shed their surroundings and appearances with a solid and persistent effort.

At one point in my journey, I was walking the streets of New York City during a hurricane as a homeless, mentally ill crackhead. After finding shelter in a seedy cross between a gallery (a place for shooting up drugs with used needles) and an hourly motel, my first objective was to meet up with a female friend and fellow druggie. As a testament to how low I was at this point in my then-forty years, after this experience, l called my mother for bus fare home. A friend in my hometown allowed me to stay at his house.

My experience at this point is summarized by another saying I am fond of: "Wherever you go, there you are!"

While a change of environment can help to a limited extent, it takes acceptance of reality to facilitate real change. At my mother's suggestion, I enrolled in a drug treatment program, though at the time, it was only my need for shelter that compelled me, as I had exhausted the patience of my friend who was letting me stay with him. He was through with my lack of willingness to help myself. In retrospect, having me leave his home was a life-saving act. Fortunately, there was a dorm in the Salvation Army for the homeless and mentally ill.

When I moved into the rehab facility, I decided that I was going to focus on the man in the mirror, as I had hit rock bottom. The good news was that when you have hit bottom, the only way to go is up. As a prodigal son, I once had a joyous life filled with love in a nurturing environment, so I had the point of reference to know there was a better way for me to live. Even more, many others didn't have the good fortune and advantages I did in my upbringing.

My mother and father did their best to raise their six children, and though they weren't always financially secure, I grew up with a degree of wealth compared to many.

I've taken the rough experiences, the inner growth and introspection that helped me, and my extensive reading on related matters and turned that into a burning desire to help myself, those around me, and everyone I can reach through my writing.

As time passed, my desire to achieve what at times seemed to be an unattainable goal gained strength. This desire became so deeply entrenched in my life and psyche that I began to consider it a worthy obsession—a justification for living and a way to bring honor to my predecessors and descendants. My passion for self-help raised my self-esteem, enhanced my financial situation, and bolstered my overall well-being.

The pain and effort of the most successful people of our time have led to significant rewards. To that end, life will give back what you put into it. It takes overcoming many difficulties to reach a lofty goal. The loftier the goal, the more work and problems come with it, but the more worthwhile it is.

The following examples show how having a Magnificent Obsession will pay dividends:

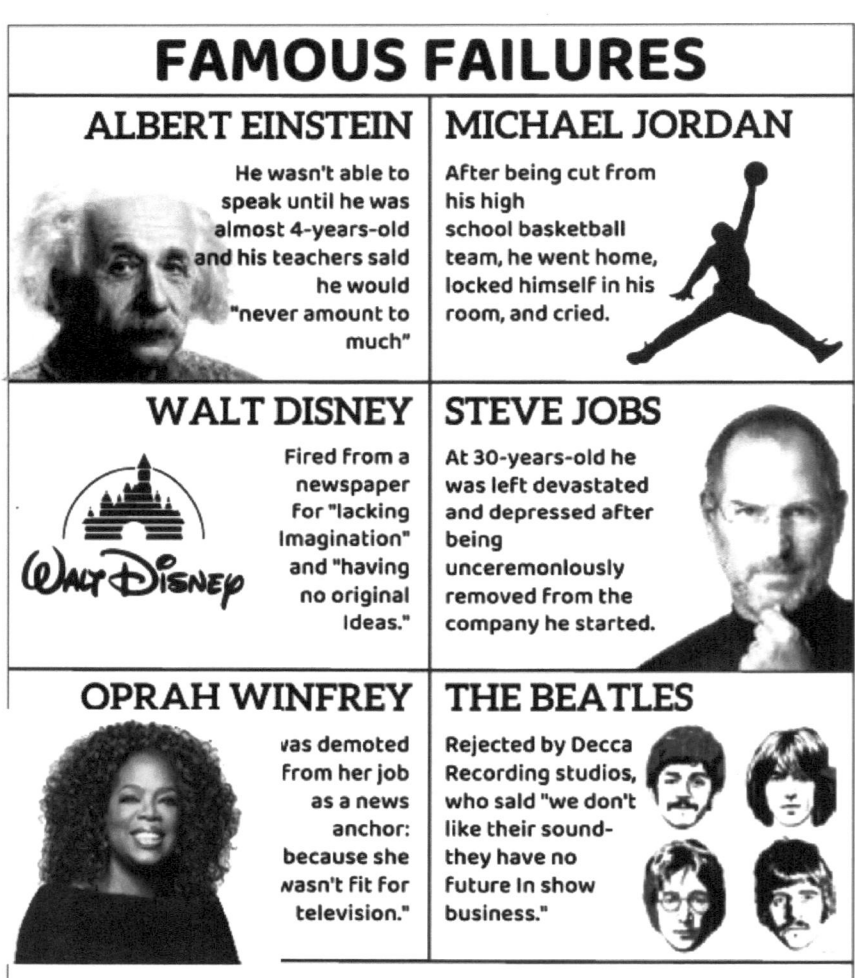

FAMOUS FAILURES

ALBERT EINSTEIN

He wasn't able to speak until he was almost 4-years-old and his teachers said he would "never amount to much"

MICHAEL JORDAN

After being cut from his high school basketball team, he went home, locked himself in his room, and cried.

WALT DISNEY

Fired from a newspaper for "lacking Imagination" and "having no original Ideas."

STEVE JOBS

At 30-years-old he was left devastated and depressed after being unceremoniously removed from the company he started.

OPRAH WINFREY

vas demoted from her job as a news anchor: because she wasn't fit for television."

THE BEATLES

Rejected by Decca Recording studios, who said "we don't like their sound- they have no future In show business."

IF YOU'VE NEVER FAILED, YOU'VE NEVER TRIED ANYTHING NEW

Each one of these people had a calling and faced significant obstacles along the way. This example shows how invaluable a Magnificent Obsession can be, resulting in realities you never thought possible.

Always remember "A winner never quits and a quitter never wins."

I want to reiterate the fact that each one of these people had a calling and faced significant obstacles along the way. This example shows how invaluable a Magnificent Obsession can be, resulting in realities you never thought possible.

Always remember "A winner never quits and a quitter never wins."

You dont have to be great to start, but you have to start to be great.

How badly do you want what your mind tells you to go after?

WHAT CAN WE DO ABOUT OUR PAST MISTAKES?

No one has ever existed who has not made a mistake or error in judgment. The problem is not acknowledging that one made a mistake before making amends. Is it possible to heal the harm without knowing that one did harm? We first must be aware of the misstep to reduce the likelihood of repeating it. After considering the best way to move forward without further harm, re-establishing a harmonious situation is possible.

> KARMA is real. You can't keep doing people dirty and being a complete asshole and think God is going to bless you. It may not be today or tomorrow or next week but what goes around comes back around and when that bitch come back for you it'll be tenfold.

If any individual has a fault, it doesn't help them to speak or act negatively towards another. This idea is especially true when striving for a higher plane of existence or attempting to elevate oneself within one's sphere of influence.

In other words, one should never try to elevate themselves by speaking disparagingly of another. That is especially true when the comments are not well founded, and the only intent is to harm the others character and reputation.

SUMMARY

In this brief memoir, I, Andrew S. Majors strive to inspire and uplift those who have or are undergoing addiction and or mental health issues. Because of having overcome the difficulties that accompany those afflictions, I believe my insights and lessons learned to better cope, have been succinctly articulated in this booklet to be an invaluable tool for anyone involved in seeking to lessen or potentially temporarily overcome those challenges.

It is sincerely my belief that once addicted, you're always addicted and must always be on guard to avoid relapses. However, with the thought that "time heals all wounds," just "saying no" gets easier.

For those that acknowledge the need for assistance in dealing with psychosis, please adopt the thinking that coping with mental health issues by all affected (family & friends) and being highly functional is within the attainment of mostly all that acknowledge their issues and have a desire/want to improve themselves!

Author/Spokesman

www.ingramcontent.com/pod-product-compliance
Lightning Source LLC
Chambersburg PA
CBHW040902120626
46551CB00001B/126